Dating Advice

Flirting Tips And Relationship Strategies For Women To Captivate And Evoke Desire In Men

(To Comprehend His Nature, Engender A Profound Attachment Within Him And Captivate His Affections)

Alvaro Carey

TABLE OF CONTENT

Good Relationship Communication 1

Living Is What It Means To Be A Woman 6

Comprehending The Dating Environment 15

The Significance Of Closeness In Establishing Robust Bonds 29

The Real Deal With Internet Dating 43

Steroid-Fueled Seduction On Facebook 63

Inform Someone Of Your Whereabouts 73

Where To Look For Love 87

Selecting A Date 98

Take Initiative Rather Than Reacting 108

Good Relationship Communication

Communication is one of the most crucial elements of any relationship, romantic or otherwise. Understanding how to communicate successfully is crucial since how you speak with your partner can make or ruin your relationship.

It helps couples to get along, understand one another, and establish a strong emotional bond. Learning to communicate well is essential for being a good girlfriend. It entails being an excellent listener, being honest and open with your thoughts and feelings, resolving disagreements healthily and productively, and showing empathy and understanding for your partner.

Let's get into more depth about each of these points:

I. Acquire Effective Listening Techniques

Hearing what your spouse says is not the only aspect of listening. It also involves understanding their viewpoint, paying attention, and demonstrating interest. It is possible to get better at listening with patience and practice.

The following advice will help you improve as a listener:

1. Steer clear of distractions. Put your phone away, switch off the TV, and give your lover your attention when he speaks to you. Look him in the eye and offer him your whole attention.

2. Avoid Interrupting. Give your companion time to complete their thinking before answering. Wait to offer counsel or your ideas until they specifically ask for it. Honor their freedom to express themselves completely.

3. Make inquiries. Ask open-ended inquiries that entice your companion to go into further detail about their emotions, ideas, and experiences to demonstrate your attention and curiosity. In other words, rather than enquiring, "Did you have a good day?" ask, "What was the best part of your day?" and "How did you feel about that meeting?"

Summarise and paraphrase. To ensure you understand and pay attention, repeat what your spouse stated in your own words. Saying, "So what you are saying is..." or "Let me see if I got this right..." are two examples of what you can say.

5. Provide an assessment. Positive feedback is a great way to show your partner how much you appreciate and support them. Say something like, "I'm glad you told me that." and "That sounds exciting." and "I'm proud of you for doing that."

II. Be Open And Honest In Expressing Your Thoughts And Feelings

Since communication is two-way, it's critical to express your ideas and feelings with your spouse in addition to listening to them.

● Be Particular And Explicit. Express yourself clearly and simply in your message. Steer clear of statements that could mislead or confuse your companion. Say, "I'm feeling sad because..." or "I'm happy because..." instead of "I'm fine," for example.

Implement "I" Statements. You must learn to express yourself honestly and accept responsibility for your needs and feelings if you want to be a good girlfriend. Don't use "you" phrases to criticize or place blame on your partner because this could make them feel defensive or assaulted. As opposed to expressing, "You never listen to me," stating, "I feel ignored when you don't pay attention to me," or even "I need you to listen to me more."

● Act with decency and constructiveness. Make thoughtful word choices and refrain from using cruel or abusive language, which might strain your connection. Never curse, belittle, or disparage your partner. Don't discuss problems or errors from the past that don't relate to the present circumstance. Pay attention to the here and now, and prioritize solving issues above creating new ones.

● Be Firm Without Being Rude. Being assertive entails speaking up for oneself and politely expressing your needs and desires. Conversely, aggression entails pushing your opinions on others and going against their rights or limits. Aggression can erode a relationship, but assertiveness can build one. For example, you may say, "I would appreciate it if you could do this for me," or, "Can we compromise on this?" as opposed to, "You have to do this for me."

● Be Receptive To Input: Since communication is not one-way or two-way, be receptive to your partner's viewpoint. Refrain from reacting angrily or defensively after getting criticism.

What Qualifies a Woman As Such?

Although it's not as simple as a-b-c, being a woman is also not that hard. These are some things about being a woman that you should know.

Living Is What It Means To Be A Woman

The power to procreate is the pinnacle of femininity. Maternity is the pinnacle of femininity. Being a mother is the best definition of a woman there is. Giving birth to a kid is not the sole aspect of being a mother.

It entails a woman guiding, loving, and caring for the child as they grow up to be the man or woman they should be—raising the child to the best they can be. Every individual has a mother of his own.

One of the main reasons men should always be grateful for women is the struggle of bearing a kid for nine months in the womb and the agony of giving birth.

B. Feminineness Is Essential to Being a Woman

Women are shaped like curves. Men are infatuated with a woman's voluptuous curves, a masterpiece in and of themselves. But being a lady entails more than just having attractive features.

Being feminine entails doing all of these things guilt-free:

Taking longer showers.

Taking hot bubble baths.

Wearing sexy knickers in any color or style.

Lighting scented candles.

Get your hair done and colored to suit your mood.

Experimenting with nail polish colors that suit your nails.

Shaving your legs and underarms.

Wearing heels and perfume and applying makeup.

Why? Merely because these items are made to complement your feminine taste and nature, and you are a woman.

C: Being a woman entails having strong emotions

Emotional beings, we women. Women are dominant when it comes to feeling.

One of the benefits of being a woman is having the freedom to feel emotions. No matter where you are or when you feel like crying, you are free to do so. You can cry aloud, and no one will blame or judge you. You can shout until you feel like you've had enough, and no one will stop you if you do.

You can laugh aloud and chuckle with your friends when you're joyful. You are free to express your fear. Your face will exude affection if you're in it. One of the main distinctions between men and women is this. Nowhere can men cry. They must always keep their emotions in check. Women are weak, defenseless beings. It is precisely this vulnerability that defines a woman as such.

D: The Right to Speak Because I Am a Woman

Women tend to talk a lot from birth. Though some men may find it bothersome, I simply cannot envision a world in which women did not converse and laugh with one another. Watching women conversing and laughing with one another is energizing and lovely. It would simply be too dull in a world without women.

Women can discuss any topic. Women can chat nonstop. Nobody else can get away with doing this. A man does not become any more of a man by talking a lot. It's just not his style.

E-Looking Hot in Anything Is Part of Being a Woman

Women can still look extremely attractive and sensual when dressed like males. Men are seldom attractive when dressed as women. That is the benefit of being a female. From jeans to polo shirts, dresses, gowns, skirts, pants, costumes, shorts, sneakers, rubber shoes, sandals, high heels, boots, slippers, hats, tiaras, shades, contacts, belts, swimsuits, to nothing at all, women can wear anything.

Any outfit a woman chooses will make her look gorgeous and seductive. She can be girly, basic, hip, punk, formal, or casual.

F - Selecting Love Is Part of Being a Woman

Being allowed to select the man she wants to love and reject those who don't suit her preferences is one of the benefits of being a woman. First to make decisions are women. Men court women.

Receiving gifts from guys is a perk of being a lady. Men will approach you if you're a lady. It also signifies that guys will look at her with curiosity.

A man will undoubtedly be rejected if a woman doesn't like him, regardless of how attractive or flawless he appears to be. A woman can make decisions.

Chapter 2: How to Choose the Ideal Partner

Using a dating service for the first several hours or even days can be annoying. Recall that you're new and that not many people will have had an opportunity to view your profile. Therefore, don't be offended if you don't receive many requests and messages immediately. Use this time to reflect on what you want in a match and to keep updating and enhancing your profile.

Everyone would naturally love to find a prosperous, attractive, and romantic mate. Since you've lived in this world for some time, you know that wealth can disappear, beauty can wane, and a good job doesn't always translate into excellent character. Consider the qualities of a potential spouse that are less evident but far more significant. You may always start with similar hobbies or a sense of humor, and you'll quickly discover your interests.

This may be your chance to reconsider your past decisions regarding your love life and to go out and meet some new individuals. Your choices haven't worked out, so you're searching for a mate. Examine any trends in your previous relationships to see whether they are a factor in the current issue.

List the attributes you value in a mate, but don't go overboard. Just because someone doesn't play professional football or has a graduate degree shouldn't be reason enough to rule out a possible match. A book shouldn't be judged by its cover. Both you and your possible mates have more to offer than what may ever fit your profile.

Consider the following, and make a note of what you want from each option:

-Observes
-Profession -Passions/Interests
- Feelings

-Your desires in a relationship and their desires in a relationship -Gripes

Take a look at that list. If one of you is seeking something serious and the other is just looking to have fun, finding a match with your favorite eye color won't help you bridge the gap. You may have thought that appearance was the most significant criterion.

Although you have undoubtedly considered these ideas previously, writing them down helps you determine whether or not they are critical attributes. Be advised that your choices will be taken into account by several dating site algorithms. More blonde profiles will appear in your feed if you click on many of them.

Online dating allows you to date folks you wouldn't ordinarily meet. A huge number of individuals from diverse backgrounds populate these websites. Of course, not all of them hang around in the same spots as you. Through these sites, you can meet folks you might not have otherwise given much thought to.

Don't be too hard on the images. We all wake up one day and find that our muscles are less toned or we have more wrinkles than before. Don't make decisions based only on practical considerations; show them the civility you want to show them.

Online dating services allow you to meet new and intriguing people in a safe setting. You might act like a kid at a candy store, but you won't have the distractions of a bar or sporting event. Conversing with matches with interests that diverge from your own. Talking to multiple individuals at once is quite acceptable. Don't overburden yourself, though. You could get numbed by the sheer quantity of possible pairings. With 1.6 billion swipes on Tinder alone each day, you don't want to take a too casual attitude. While you should appreciate each Tinder match you receive, keep in mind that there have been 26 billion matches made globally.

Comprehending The Dating Environment

To navigate the dating industry properly, it's essential to comprehend the modern dating scene. This part will examine the difficulties and trends of modern dating and assist you in differentiating between positive and negative relationship dynamics.

3.1 Contemporary Dating Practices and Issues

a. Online dating: As technology has advanced, online dating has grown in popularity. Although it's a practical method of meeting possible mates, it may also be overwhelming. When utilizing dating apps or services, exercise caution, take your time, and put your security first.

b. Ghosting: Ghosting is someone abruptly ceasing all correspondence without a reason.

It's a typical problem in contemporary dating. Keep in mind that it conveys more about the other person's communication and maturity than it does about your value.

c. Mixed Signals: A major problem sometimes is a lack of communication. It's important to have frank discussions with others about your intentions and expectations since sometimes people will give you confusing signals.

d. Time management: It might be difficult to juggle dating, work, school, and social life. Ensure you're allocating time for personal development and self-care, and be aware of your priorities.

3.2 Handling the Culture of Hookupsvs Long-Term Partnerships

a. Make Your Intentions Clear: Be sure you know what you want before committing to any relationship. Tell people the truth if you're looking for casual relationships. Be honest about your goal for a long-term relationship as well.

b. Communication and Consent: In the culture of hookups, candid communication and consent are essential. Make sure you and your partner are always comfortable with the degree of closeness involved.

c. Emotional Safety: The hookup culture can occasionally muddle the distinction between emotional and physical relationships. Recognize and express your emotional limits with clarity.

d. Long-Term Relationship Objectives: Spend time getting to know possible partners well if you seek a committed relationship. The foundation of enduring partnerships is mutual respect, communication, and shared beliefs.

Chapter 2: Comprehending Attraction

Different Attraction Types

Understanding the many types of attraction can offer important insights into the dating process, as attraction results from a complex interplay of various elements. Physical, emotional, and intellectual attraction are the three main attraction categories.

Physical Attraction: This describes your initial attraction to someone based only on their outward appearance. It considers things like physical form, facial traits, and general attractiveness.

Even though physical attraction plays a significant role, it's critical to understand that it's only one component of a healthy partnership.

Emotional Attraction: This type of attraction is centered on how well people connect and get along emotionally. It entails understanding and empathy as well as comparable interests and beliefs. Building strong and meaningful connections requires emotional attraction.

Intellectual Attraction: Mental compatibility, engaging dialogues, and common interests are the foundations of intellectual attraction. It entails challenging and engaging your partner's mind, which can strengthen your relationship and increase your chances of being compatible in the long run.

The Attraction Science

There is more to attraction than just human preference; science also supports this theory. Several biological and psychological variables influence attraction.

Physical Cues: Some physical cues are generally considered appealing, such as symmetrical facial features, good physical health, and well-groomed habits. These cues frequently signal reproductive potential and genetic fitness.

Similarity: Individuals are drawn to those who share their beliefs, attitudes, passions, and experiences. In relationships, commonalities foster a feeling of comfort and ease.

Non-Verbal Communication: Body language, proximity, and eye contact are examples of non-verbal clues important in determining attractiveness. Determining interest and establishing a relationship can be facilitated by understanding and comprehending nonverbal cues.

Increasing Physical Appealingness

Even though physical appearance is only one component of attraction, first impressions can be influenced by it. Improving your physical appearance doesn't alter who you are; instead, it means putting your best foot forward.

Personal Hygiene: Maintain a look that expresses your personality, practice good hygiene, and dress nicely. Maintaining proper hygiene can greatly improve your appearance and self-esteem.

Health and Fitness: Maintain a healthy lifestyle and partake in frequent exercise. Exercise enhances your physical well-being and overall beauty in addition to your confidence.

Individual Style: Create a style that expresses your uniqueness and fits your personality. Consider the occasion and wear something that makes you feel confident and at ease.

Understanding that physical appearance is not a prerequisite for a happy and rewarding relationship is crucial. True compatibility and connection depend on more than surface-level attraction; they also depend on emotional and cognitive characteristics.

In the upcoming chapter, we will explore good communication techniques as they are essential for establishing rapport, expressing interest, and cultivating long-lasting partnerships.

Chapter 3: How to Write a Profile for Dating

Advice on crafting a catchy title for a dating profile

Potential partners will first see your dating profile headline, so creating a strong impression is critical. These pointers can help you create a catchy headline for your dating profile:

Be concise and clear. There should be no more than 50 characters in your headline. This will guarantee that it appears on all dating apps and websites.

Be distinct. Your headline needs to be distinctive from the rest. Steer clear of cliches and overused expressions.

Be truthful. Your interests and personality should come through in your headline.

Be upbeat. Your title ought to be cheery and encouraging. It should pique the interest of possible mates in finding out more about you.

Here are some fantastic examples of headlines for dating profiles:

Adventurer searching for a co-conspirator.

A foodie looking to enjoy meals with another foodie.

Looking for a travel companion to go on adventures with throughout the world.

a Family-oriented individual seeking a lifelong partner.

Dog lover seeking playmate for fetch who is also a dog lover.

How to create a compelling bio for a dating profile

You can share more information about yourself with possible companions through your dating profile bio. Writing an interesting, educational bio that is full of personality is crucial.

The following advice might help you create a compelling bio for your dating profile:

Be sincere and real. Be authentic and truthful to yourself when writing about yourself.

Be upbeat. Your bio ought to be cheery and encouraging. It should pique the interest of possible mates in finding out more about you.

Give details. Talk about your values, interests, and hobbies. This will enable prospective partners to determine your compatibility.

Use your imagination. Tell a personal narrative about yourself in your bio. Your bio will become more captivating and memorable as a result.

Be unique. Avoid attempting to be someone you're not. Others easily recognize fakes, and they will only make you seem less appealing.

Here's an illustration of an attention-grabbing bio for a dating profile:

I'm a wanderlust person who enjoys camping, hiking, and traveling. I also love to cook at home and try out new eateries because I'm a gourmet. Someone who loves being outside, is energetic, and adventurous is what I'm searching for.

Selecting appropriate dating photos

Your headline and profile are not nearly as significant as your dating photographs. interested in getting to know you more because they are the first thing potential partners will see.

The following advice will help you select the ideal dating photos:

Select crystal-clear, well-lit pictures. Steer clear of employing dark or fuzzy photos.

Select pictures of you grinning and having a good time. Select pictures that capture your essence since positive individuals attract other positive people.

Select pictures of you doing activities you enjoy. This will assist prospective companions in determining common interests between you.

Select a range of images. This can help prospective partners better understand your appearance and identity.

When selecting dating images, keep the following in mind:

Steer clear of group shots. It might be challenging to identify yourself in a group photo, as well as challenging to spot you.

Steer clear of taking selfies. Selfies can give the impression that you are conceited and narcissistic.

Steer clear of filtered images. Photos with filters applied can make you appear fictitious and distant.

Refrain from utilizing excessively exposing photos. Something should be left up to the reader's imagination.

If you adhere to these recommendations, you can make a dating profile that will draw in possible partners.

Setting the Scene: Getting Ready for a Partnership

You have to get yourself ready for a relationship before you can find a lover who is worth your time. Nothing is worse than meeting the perfect man, but you're unprepared for him. Furthermore, a lot of women nowadays fail to take this crucial first step, which ultimately prevents them from being able to find a boyfriend. Finding oneself is essentially the first step towards finding love. Before you let someone else get to know you, you must first get to know yourself.

This chapter will teach you how to become a better self-aware person, view relationships differently, and identify the qualities you value in a partner. Let's begin by reviewing the initial steps of becoming ready for a relationship.

First, look for yourself.

Taking care of yourself is the first step in preparing for a relationship. You both need to be well for your relationship to succeed. Do you think of yourself as healthy? You must ask yourself the following questions to respond to that question: Am I getting enough sleep?

Do I regularly spend time with my loved ones and friends?

Do I eat healthily?

Do I give myself enough time to groom?

You can determine whether or not you are leading a healthy life by answering these questions. You'll see that the inquiries cover more ground than just physical well-being. They also consider how well you and your loved ones get along. Your physical and mental well-being typically impacts your relationship, so you must care for both. For instance, if you don't get enough sleep, your focus and concentration will be poor, leading to a stressful day. Your relationship may suffer as a result of this frustration.

This is the step where you should start focusing on self-improvement. For example, you should aim to sleep eight hours daily for adequate rest. This enables you to work more efficiently and creatively. You should prioritize eating items that will improve your health when it comes to eating. A lady should present herself nicely when it comes to grooming. Set aside time to pamper your face and style your hair every day.

Taking care of yourself makes you feel happy and confident since it not only keeps you healthy but also makes you feel good about yourself. You become even more alluring as a result.

Step 2: Embrace Yourself Initially

It's a well-known adage that you cannot love another person until you have loved yourself. Though cliched, it is accurate. Loving oneself is the next step. How would you go about doing that? Here are several methods for achieving that:

I respect your oddity: Do you enjoy watching scary films? Or do you enjoy making jokes so much that it becomes difficult for others to know if you are being serious or not? Accepting your eccentricities, such as the ones listed above, is one way to love who you are because they are unique. It's easier to handle feelings of shame when your prospective partner discovers your oddities and individuality when you accept them.

Honor your advantages: Every person in this world possesses some wonderful qualities. It can be singing, cooking, or solving complex equations. Discovering your strengths should help you feel more confident. Retain your self-assurance and accept yourself for it.

The Significance Of Closeness In Establishing Robust Bonds

A Firm Basis for Confidence
Trust is based on intimacy, which is its foundation. Allowing someone into your personal space—both physically and emotionally—is akin to saying, "I trust you with my vulnerability." The foundation of any long-lasting relationship is this trust. It's the conviction that you will protect your partner's private thoughts and feelings, and they will do the same for you.

It takes more than keeping secrets to rely on one another in difficult situations and know that your significant other will support you. When you trust one another, you can weather life's storms together, knowing you have a dependable friend. Furthermore, this trust strengthens the ties that bind, producing a vicious cycle of intimacy and proximity. ➚The Compost for Emotional Development
Not only is intimacy a dynamic force that fosters emotional development, but it's

also a static state of being. In a personal connection, the growth of each partner is supported. They support one another in overcoming obstacles, facing anxieties, and pursuing their goals. In this connection, you'll discover love and the chance to grow into the greatest version of yourself.

Intimate relationships provide support and encouragement, which can act as a potent stimulant for personal development. It's simpler to take chances, get out of your comfort zone, and follow your hobbies when you have a partner who believes in you, supports you, and gets inside your head. Both couples may flourish in such a setting, and as they see each other's personal growth, their bond becomes stronger.

2.3 The Value of Close Sexual Contact

In a love relationship, sexual intimacy is an essential part of overall closeness. It provides a special and incredibly satisfying dimension to the relationship between two people. Although it's not the only foundation for a solid relationship, physical intimacy is essential for strengthening emotional ties and cultivating a strong, long-lasting union. We discuss the value of sexual closeness and how it affects romantic relationships in this section.

➤ A Link Not Like Any Other

A unique link is formed between lovers through sexual contact. It's a physical means of expressing love, passion, and desire. People can connect on a very basic level by making love, which transcends words and feelings. Instilling a sense of unity and oneness with your partner can be a powerful and transcendent experience.

Dopamine and oxytocin, among other neurochemicals released in the brain due to physical proximity, enhance emotions of joy, love, and attachment. The emotional bond between lovers is strengthened via a biological process. In addition, it's a form of nonverbal communication that enables partners to express their love and desire in a way that words cannot match.

➤ Strengthening Emotional Bonds

Emotional and sexual intimacy are entwined; they support and enhance one another. An intimate and fulfilling sexual relationship between two people frequently results in a stronger emotional attachment. Emotional intimacy requires trust, vulnerability, and open communication, all fostered by sharing these private moments.

In addition, it offers a secure environment free from fear and judgment where couples can be who they truly are. Emotional connection is strengthened when people are accepted and desired in their most vulnerable state. It serves as a reminder that their partner values and adores them for their entire being, not just their physical characteristics.

Section Two

Ways to Develop Into an Alpha Female

You think you're an alpha or want to be an alpha woman, so you picked up this book. You are not born with any of the characteristics you have read about. You can develop each of these qualities inside yourself!

You may have purchased this book for all or partly due to your frustration with previous male relationships. Now, it's understandable that your confidence in dating may be low, even though it may be good in other areas.

You may have felt unloveable, unattractive, and even unworthy of a man because of past failed relationships, but none of those things are true. You likely selected the incorrect men and are not the only one. Many men and women make poor lifelong partner selections. Our high divorce rate of today serves as proof.

Confidence is an underlying component that is constant for many of the characteristics listed in the first chapter. This chapter on becoming an alpha woman will center on that. It doesn't matter if your confidence is in other areas or only in dating. You may boost your confidence in essentially the same way.

What Does Confidence Mean?

In its most fundamental form, confidence is the conviction that you can do a task. It can, therefore, differ in many aspects of your life.

If your career has been successful, you undoubtedly have a lot of confidence in your ability to do your work. If you've gotten good at a pastime like painting or photography, you probably also have a lot of confidence in it, but remember where you started.

Did you have the same confidence level when you started your new job, maybe just out of college? Perhaps you did if you had excellent grades or an internship that gave you early success, but it's unlikely that you had the same confidence level as you do now. How was it constructed?

Most likely, without even recognizing that you were doing it! You made an effort and had both achievements and setbacks. If you were unsuccessful at something, you used what you learned from it and kept trying until you reached the next level. Your confidence increased with the amount of achievement you achieved. It's a logical step you most likely took without giving confidence a second thought.

We are now focusing on developing your confidence and providing strategies. It's an intentional attempt to create something less strong than you'd like to acknowledge. Now, go ahead and acknowledge it! Like anything else, something cannot be fixed if its flaws are not initially acknowledged.

Where Do You Think Your Confidence Is?

Let's focus on four aspects of your life where confidence is needed:

Employment and professional path

Money

Relationships (individually with men, family, and friends)

You (self-talk, personal development, individual bodily and spiritual selves)

Give each region careful thought. How confident are you in your abilities to perform your job and advance in your profession in terms of your job and career?

How much faith do you have in saving, investing, spending sensibly, and managing your finances?

Divide the relationships you assess into three categories: relationships with males, relationships with your family, and relationships with friends. To what extent can you develop pleasant, healthy connections in these areas?

Lastly, you. How do you talk to yourself these days? Is it more favorable or unfavorable? Do you constantly strive for personal development? Are you in good health and working towards good goals? How confident are you spiritually?

You can identify the areas of your life that want confidence boosts by asking and responding to these questions. Finding a place to start is the first step in implementing constructive improvements.

Chapter 1: A Few Women-Related Trivia

Let's start by discussing women. The main cause of your nervousness when approaching women is your mistaken belief that women are superior to other people. Remember this, if nothing else, from this chapter: Faking it is a good thing, 2) you can't meet anyone if you chat with no one, and 3) women desire your attention.

Ladies Avoid Biting

True enough, they can be frightening. They are also capable of being cruel. Their furious stare may make you feel as little as ananobot. Before retreating into your closet and vowing never to date again until you're more "ready," remember that ladies are people like you. They're not native to Venus. They are not extraterrestrial. They are human beings with fundamental needs, desires, and wants. Why shouldn't that someone be you since they also want to spend the night with someone?

In all honesty, women are hardly the enigmatic and complex characters Hollywood loves constructing for plot-heavy feature films. Furthermore, ladies are not the stereotypical characters you read about in literature or watch on sitcoms. Women know how nerve-wracking the whole mating game—or courtship initiation, if you prefer—is. When a hot guy is around, they also become anxious. They stumble when speaking, forget what they're saying, and exhibit altered body language and flushed cheeks.

Just because someone uses a different gender pronoun than you doesn't mean you should be afraid of them. It should encourage you to approach an attractive woman rather than make you feel afraid. Perhaps, after all, she does want to speak with you. Sigh!

This is the issue. Even in 2016, starting a conversation is still considered the guy's job. Guys are still expected to approach girls. Granted, some women are brave enough to approach a guy and discuss, but most women prefer to wait for the guy to initiate contact. Why? Women seem to like alphas. Betas don't pique their curiosity. They are looking for a trustworthy man to take command and lead. By striking up that conversation, you demonstrate to her that you're not scared to be the alpha. You're demonstrating to her that, among all the guys, you don't hesitate to pursue his goals. That will appeal to her, if not outright sexy, which brings us to our next topic.

Men with Confidence Attract Women

Have you ever seen a pair who completely stun you since they are such opposites regarding attractiveness? The man is mediocre and slightly nerdy. He wears socks and sandals without shame and drives a Toyota sedan. The female is stunning and appears to be completely enamored with the guy. When you see them, you ask yourself, "How did that dude get that girl?" How on earth could a 4.5 hook up at 9? He doesn't appear to be an unrecognizable C-List actor or wealthy. It's obvious, though, that more than just chance brought them together. He didn't simply appear out of nowhere one day and ask her if she wanted to be his girlfriend.

He probably came up to her with confidence. He didn't come across as insecure when he approached her. He made an alpha move towards her. Ladies react well to alphas. That explains why strong males and jocks tend to attract girls. It's attractive when someone is at the top of their game and wants to be with you. It gives you a sense of accomplishment, and who doesn't enjoy winning?

I'm just an ordinary Joe, you may be thinking to yourself. I have no idea how to confidently approach a girl on the street. When I leave the house, I seldom ever make sure that I'm wearing trousers.

Now, here's the thing: Show confidence; whether it's fake or genuine, it doesn't matter. The proverb "Fake it until you make it" holds true here. Even though all you have to give the other sex is an outdated bag of M&Ms and pointless trivia, when you approach a girl, who you are doesn't matter as much as who you seem to be. Put simply, don't be afraid to approach her because she doesn't know you.

Although it sounds cliche, what matters most is how you express something, not what you say. It may surprise you that words make up only 7% of the enduring impression in a conversation. Five-five percent is body language. This is from Deborah Gruenfeld, whose website we strongly advise you to visit.

Nothing is at stake for you. She is unaware that you earn just $15,000 annually and live with your parents. She is unaware that you dated Jennifer Crowley during your final relationship in the ninth grade. All that counts is that you personify the guy you want her to think you are in that first exchange. You must project confidence, control over the situation, and importance in your approach if you want her to believe that. Make sure you exude that confidence when you speak with her, even if you have to write a confidence mantra on your bathroom mirror so you can see and believe it every day. Thus, when conversing with a girl, pay attention to your body language. Sustain eye contact, smile without inhibition, and maintain a calm demeanor.

Recall that your only goal is to receive a yes. You're not attempting to bind a lifelong companion. The first step is to say yes; you'll figure out the rest.

Additionally, after speaking with a female, you might decide that you no longer want to spend your valuable Netflix weekends with her, let alone get to know her. You might approach a girl with a sense of authority and confidence. She may greet you with a grin and brighten her eyes, which are universal signs that you are welcome, but she may also open her mouth and speak in a way that irritates your ears. You might want to leap off a bridge when you hear her giggle. Alternatively, you'll see that she has a lot of facial hair up close. Though everyone has their deal breakers, is there anything wrong with dating a woman who is marginally more hairy than the typical human mammal?

The Real Deal With Internet Dating

Some still see Online dating as taboo, something you shouldn't truly discuss with your peers. When you connect with someone online, you simply make up a backstory to share with them. But in the dating world, online dating has gained popularity, and many women use it to locate a mate. The fact that many women are now using the internet to discover their soul mate is not surprising. There are benefits to employing this approach, such as the fact that it doesn't require you to go out and is less awkward. How does going on an online date feel like, then? Is this the only answer to the modern problem of finding the perfect partner? Or is this just another method for women to learn about the negative aspects and difficulties of dating? Before discussing the dating success guidelines, let's keep in mind that, similar to other dating methods.

Advantages

You may be positive that everyone you meet when dating online is single.

Additionally, there are plenty of options; the days of going out to clubs alone and hoping to find someone decently handsome are long gone. With online dating, you may choose from thousands of guys with various origins, appearances, occupations, ages, and hobbies, and all it takes is one click to express interest.

In online dating, you are also in control of everything. If you've gone out with a group of guys in a pub, you'll find that you wind up lowering your standards to find someone, as not all of them will be interested in you or be truly single. If you look it up online, this is not the case. You can choose to respond to a few, ignore the majority, and consider dating a handful of the hundreds of guys who have reached out to you here.

Before heading out on a date, you can also ask the guy questions—of course, in a discreet and non-grill manner. You might inquire about their fundamental beliefs, political opinions, and favorite movies, songs, and pastimes. If things don't work out in the end, it's also simple to break up with a candidate—without the drama of having a mutual friend set you up on a date. Once you exclude a person from your list of possible matches, he will simply vanish from the online dating scene, freeing you to look at your next option.

Online multi-dating is also an option. It's quite difficult to avoid going on multiple dates. There's no use being fascinated with just one person since you'll still be conversing, looking at images, and texting other possible dates even though you're not seeing two people simultaneously. Since someone else will let you know he is in a message format, you are less likely to fall in love with someone immediately or lose your mind if you discover that he isn't into you in this situation!

Cons

The reality that you aren't truly seeing the person you are dating is unavoidable. They just share a photo on their profile, so it's up to you to determine whether or not you like him. Most of the time, photos can be deceptive. In addition to the fact that people normally appear better in photos than they do in person due to factors like lighting, angles, and shadows, there are other characteristics of people that are impossible to discern from a single image, such as height, build, or if they have really small hands. Therefore, let me remind you to avoid profiles with little photographs. Though there are very few certainties, it is preferable to have more images available.

There's also the possible date's chemistry with you to think about. Being perfectly OK over email is not the same as being perfectly fine in person. Yes, your date may be an Adonis, and you may have had amazing email correspondence for some time, but when you meet him in person, there's just no chemistry, and you can't help but worry about how you'll get through the evening with him.

Additionally, dating online will make you incredibly picky. You may begin with very low standards at first, but as time passes, your standards will rise to the point where they are nearly impossible to meet. It's difficult to overcome the fact that no one will be suitable for you shortly.

Also, there is your rivalry. You compete online against ladies from various walks of life and worldwide. You may be one of several attractive women down the pub, if not the only one. On the internet, however, thousands of attractive women are presenting their wares, including their talents and appealing features, and flirting with each other. Be aware that there are more attractive women than males on the internet. Indeed, that might irritate you.

Additionally, it is time-consuming online dating. It can rule your life! You'll receive messages from guys who like you, and you'll have to like them back. Just before your date with another guy, one guy gives you his number, and another will call you for a conversation. You still have to consider your life, friends, and job in addition to that. At this point, your brain might as well burst.

Not every man you meet online wants to be in a relationship. They may not truly seek a committed relationship just because they seek dates. Some guys you'll encounter are only dating their way out of a past relationship because they haven't moved on from it. Some have been through so much suffering that they must harm a few women to go on. On the other hand, some only consider internet dating a quick and simple way to hook up and don't desire anything serious. Therefore, find out as soon as possible about his past relationships before moving on to the next level with a potential date.

Internet dating has ups and downs, just like any other way of meeting possible companions. Before you start reading advice on discovering the right man for you, it's crucial to understand both facets of the industry!

What a Female Truly Desires

Thus, if you've spent decades being turned down by women, you most likely have an extremely skewed perception of them. It's likely that you blame all women and believe that they are the source of your problems because they don't understand you.

I had the most basic insight of all time one day. "It must have something to do with what I was doing if all my friends were getting women to like them, and I wasn't," I reasoned. Therefore, I wanted to know what characteristics of my personality made the women react to me in such a snotty and frigid manner.

The issue was that I believed all women were drawn to jerks, so I reasoned that if I behaved badly, all women would like me. The truth is that she will be more than eager to talk to you if you express interest in her and demonstrate that you're sex-worthy (meaning that you're deliberate, in control, flowing, and self-amused). Remember that the way you behave and the outcomes you achieve have shaped your reality.

I'm going to discuss a few of the characteristics of personalities that appeal to women. When you're with a lady, you don't have to put on a front (remember congruence but lean a bit over the edge).

To begin with, though, you should try to emphasize some aspects of your personality while downplaying others. We've discussed it before, and I'll say it again: alpha conduct is unquestionably the first quality a woman finds attractive. It is ingrained in women's programming to be drawn to a man who can play the part of the male.

The second personality characteristic is that of an aggressive, risk-taking, and ambitious guy. A man with ambition, who isn't afraid to chase his dreams despite all obstacles, is incredibly attractive to women. That's a man who truly knows how to live his life. Avoid being the person who spends their entire day playing video games, has no life ambitions, eats bad food, and never leaves the house. Women adore a man who sees opportunity everywhere and doesn't perceive any barriers in his path. A passionate man symbolizes a lust for life and a thirst.

The third one is a kind man. This guy is different from the needy, supplicant, or pushover guy. Don't give off the impression that you are needy and want something from her in return (searching for that validation).

Men have an insatiable passion for women. You may have heard that all male accomplishments are due to women. Men allegedly go to great lengths to win over women. Yes, this is what the losers do to gain no credit. You must be willing to take chances in life since doing so will increase your attractiveness to women and teach you to embrace rather than dread life. It will determine whether or not you are willing to take risks, which is why you need to have confidence. It will determine your level of resolve in the face of failure. Don't depend on other people's approval or worry about what others think of you. You won't take on much danger if you do it.

Think of your risk tolerance as the amount you will forfeit to accomplish your objectives.

What relevance does this have to getting ahead with women, then? Indeed, many males lack a true understanding of how things operate. They believe any lady they approach would reject them and that they're just a guy making advances (Remember: Make positive assumptions). The issue is their reluctance to approach a lady and take the chance of being harmed. You have to acknowledge that you might end up dating your ideal woman. For the most part, the possibility surpasses the risk. Thus, you need to be aware of these opportunities that are right in front of you. Even while it seems simple, you won't find it easy once you discover how distorted your perception of reality has become.

But always keep this in mind:

Live for oneself.

An alpha male must put his own needs first. You have to communicate your feelings if you have them. You must communicate some aspects of your personality. If you're not being who you are by that, you don't want to live your entire life doing what a lady wants.

Chapter 5: The Art of Dialogue

Interesting Conversation Topics & Narration

Section 1: Crafting Intentional Talks

In the busy city of Connectville, James found that genuine discussion was necessary to connect with people. He saw that telling engaging stories and having deep discussions prepared the environment for genuine friendships.

Find Common Interests: James discovered that scanning possible mates' profiles for shared passions, hobbies, and interests is a good idea. Conversations about these topics quickly produced points of agreement.

Current Events and Culture: James thought discussing social trends, recent events, and common experiences would be beneficial. These topics opened opportunities for astute trades and understanding one another's perspectives.

Section 2: The Narrative's Power

Sharing Personal Experiences: James realized that telling unique tales was a powerful way to create a deeper connection. He tries to develop weakness by delving deeply into his experiences and emotions.

Relatable Anecdotes: James' contemplations and sentiments. used captivating tales to illustrate his

establishing and utilizing a more consistent flow of conversation.

Section 3: Listening intently and responding with empathy

Paying Close Attention: James practiced paying full attention, concentrating only on his conversation partner. He followed up with questions and genuinely expressed interest in their experiences and points of view.

James sympathized with his companion's feelings and responded in a way that validated his experiences. He understood that empathetic responses fostered more relationships and confidence.

Tasks and Thoughts:

Find Common Interests: Look through the profiles of potential matches to find commonalities in hobbies or interests. To utilize as icebreakers, jot down some typical objectives.

Practice Telling Stories: Choose a personal experience or tale to share with possible mates. Consider the emotions and experiences that you can convey by telling the story.

Improve Active Listening: Engage in a conversation with a friend or family member and practice paying close attention. Think about how your listening skills affect the discussion's tone.

Important lessons learned:

Establish Common Ground: Establish fast connections and start conversations about hobbies, recent advancements, and common interests. Tell Personal Tales: Telltales to elicit emotions, experiences, and thoughts while promoting new connections.

Practice Active Listening: To create meaningful and captivating conversations, concentrate, ask thoughtful questions, and respond compassionately.

To promote trustworthy associations, narrating and including discourse themes are essential strategies. This section explains the value of exchanging personal stories, having stimulating conversations, and paying close attention to conversations that resonate and create long-lasting relationships.

7. How To Get What You Desire From Guys

Because of their differences, men and women have different ways of thinking. This implies that for you as a woman to get what you want from men—including their attention, affection, and commitment—you must understand how the male mentality functions. If you typically have problems attracting guys, you might inadvertently radiate energy that turns them away.

You should put the following into practice to change things:

* Act obstinately
* Show depth and intellect
* Maintain a mystique

* Have fun
* Look, killer
* Attend to your look
* Play with your body's emotions

Play assiduously to win.

A woman who seems desperate can be one of the things that makes men take her for granted. Men enjoy a good challenge, so if you start chasing after a lady, you are relinquishing the challenge. You must remain calm, keep him guessing, and keep things low-key. You will ultimately get what you want from men because of your remarkable status, which can compel them to want you even more.

Be enigmatic

Letting men figure you out is a big part of attracting them to you. Don't divulge every little detail of your life or your sentiments to them. Additionally, you shouldn't always make yourself available. He'll start to miss your companionship and wonder where you are and what you are doing.

Show them you are deep and intelligent enough to get your desired.

In case you were unaware, intellect is attractive. It's crucial to be intelligent, know what you want, and how to achieve it to draw in men wherever you go. You can demonstrate your depth to a man by showcasing your intelligence. More than anything else, this will effectively operate to attract guys.

Don't be dull; be enjoyable.

Find out what makes guys happy, then make yourself enjoyable. This is where most women make mistakes because it is crucial despite its seeming simplicity. Jokes, sports, relaxation, video games, and making every effort to partake in what he enjoys are all recommended.

Take Good Care Of Your Look

It's time to change if you're not good at caring for yourself since attractive women attract attractive men. Make sure to apply scented deodorant, wash your teeth well, and take a shower with fragrant soaps. Always wear well-groomed hair, own a sweet-smelling perfume, and, most importantly, project immense confidence in yourself.

Put on a killer outfit.

Your clothing should always make you feel seductive. Honor yourself because your style conveys who you are. Your clothes should fit your body well and emphasize your physique. Remember that males are visual learners, so make the most of vivid hues like red or pink.

Engage In Light Body Language

While you are close, bend your body toward him, touch his hand or shoulder, lean in close, show genuine interest in what he is saying, and even smile. But don't overdo it or draw too much attention to yourself—let your actions speak for themselves.

Never forget that self-assurance is a wardrobe unto itself. Even when you look amazing, when you lack confidence, you somehow come across as nude. Always maintain your dignity since it will enable you to get what you want from men.

8. The Basics Of Mating And Dating In The Modern World

The rules of dating and mating haven't altered that much, despite the dating landscape having significantly changed in recent years due to social media platforms, dating sites, casual hook-up apps, and other developments. Men and women still perform the same dance in an attempt to establish emotional and even sexual intimacy.

Regarding the "do's" and "don'ts" of love, the guidelines often adapt to the involved people.

Nonetheless, no matter where you go, a few basic laws practically always remain the same. These easy-to-follow guidelines will make it easier for today's busy lady to navigate the murky waters of dating and mating.

Do Not Withhold Information

In the past, women used to have to wait for their ideal suitor to approach them. Because their wrists had to be tied behind their backs out of politeness, sometimes this happened too slowly, and other times it never happened.

These previous restrictions are less restrictive in the modern world. Now that women have greater authority, they can approach any guy they like and ask him out.

A woman should never hesitate to express her desires, whether for a committed relationship, a one-night encounter, or a casual friendship. Therefore, don't feel pressured to just wait. Being forthright is valued and, in certain cases, expected of a modern woman.

Do Take Notes From Past Errors

All have experienced at some time:

* Had a really bad date
* Watched the love of their life escape their grasp
* Had their hearts been wounded
* Had a terrible relationship with someone for them

The one thing that everyone should remember from these previous events is the lessons and mistakes learned. One will inevitably make the same mistakes over and over again if they do not learn from them. Dating is challenging enough without self-defeating habits that come from repetition.

Steroid-Fueled Seduction On Facebook

As you read this book, there are currently more than 1,600 million Facebook users. Research indicates that almost 50% of these consumers are female. We're talking about more than 800 million women, dude!

These women make up a sizable portion of the population who are attractive, unmarried, and accessible. But perhaps most crucially, they are addicted to Facebook, using it anytime they have a few minutes to spare. Everywhere I go, I can't help but notice attractive women using their phones to check their Facebook accounts while drinking coffee, using the gym's treadmill, or waiting in line at the supermarket.

And when they're out having fun with their pals, I watch them snap hot photos and post them to their accounts. When I see women in public, I only see this. Women use Facebook for absurdly long periods in the comfort of their homes.

If you use Facebook as often as I did, your interactions with pals mostly consist of messaging one other and leaving comments on and "liking" each other's photos. Occasionally, you might encounter a gorgeous girl with whom you have a "mutual friend" relationship. You decide to go over her profile and photos and maybe even attempt to add her to your list of friends. However, you've probably discovered that you won't get very far if you attempt to converse with one of those "random" gals.

The fact is that too many other guys are vying for her attention by sending her messages regularly, commenting on her photos, and trying to kiss her behind her back and stroke her ego. With this, how are you meant to compete? She views you as simply another irrational, lustful stranger she meets online.

Then there were the girls I had first met in person, either through my job or my social network, or girls I would talk to when out at bars or parties. I always made it a point to get their Facebook address if they were cute, just so I could stay in touch with them virtually. If you don't know how to "cut through the noise," it's difficult.

I have totally altered that circumstance during the past few months. Even though I don't spend much time on social media sites like Facebook, every time I log in, I see many nice messages from women. Some of them are people I've slept with in the past, some are in my current social circle, and some are people I haven't met yet, but I know I'll be in my bed eventually.

Additionally, meeting new ladies no longer feels like a tough, stressful task when I want to do it; it feels more like a game. I have a unique way of going through the profiles and figuring out which girls are "good to go"—the ones I know I can attract with a few basic moves and routines.

All of this is a result of my discovery of numerous Facebook seduction techniques. You can essentially "hack" this social network and use it as your matchmaking service, with thousands of women at your disposal.

I am referring to the usage of certain Facebook features for seduction, most of which users are unaware of. To make it simple for you to approach women who might otherwise ignore you and initiate flirtatious conversations that result in in-person hookups. These girls don't need to be added to your list of friends (yes, there are ways to "friend" attractive girls, even if they typically decline approaches from strangers).

All you have to do is apply the techniques I'll reveal in this chapter to log into your Facebook account. You can browse through the girls you wish to meet and set up dates in brief messages once you've done this.

Recall that you do not want to become one of the millions of other males who merely use Facebook to creep women out and don't know the "rules of the game." You don't want to be the person who makes ladies adjust their privacy settings to "private" and destroys everything for everyone else. Facebook is a crowded, buzzing place where people's attention spans are short. Typically, you will only get one opportunity to get things right.

Section Four

Having Face-to-Face Conversations

The dating game might get increasingly challenging as men age. The best approach to meeting a possible spouse is still through in-person interactions, but older men might need to lower their expectations. Older guys might learn tips from this chapter on approaching and interacting with individuals in person. It will go over how to come across well, strike up a conversation, and keep a positive outlook. Older men can succeed in dating if they take the proper attitude. neglect to make time for discovering new locations and interacting with new people. Thankfully, there are still many opportunities for older guys to network in person. Here are some pointers for looking for chances to socialize with new people:

Participate in Local Events: Networking at local events is a terrific opportunity to meet new people. Joining a book club, volunteering at a nearby charity, or going to a local event are just a few ways to meet like-minded people.

2. Join a Club: Attending a club is a terrific method to network with new individuals. passions by joining a club focused on your pastime or a local sports team.

3. Enroll in a Class: Enrolling in a class is a fantastic method to network. You're sure to find a class that interests you because there are many options. You and the other students in the class will also share a shared interest.

4. Go to Networking Events: Meeting new people in person is a terrific method to network. The purpose of these gatherings is to assist professionals in expanding their networks and forming new relationships. Make sure to attend a couple of the many networking events available in your region.

5. Give Online Dating a Try: Meeting new individuals in person might be facilitated by online dating. Although putting

yourself out there could be scary; there are lots of trustworthy and secure websites that can assist you in finding possible partners. Just remember to proceed with caution when you are meeting someone new.

6. Give Speed Dating a Try: This is a fantastic method to meet many people quickly. It's worth considering because it's an enjoyable and stress-free approach to meeting possible dates.

Older guys can discover many possibilities to meet new people face-to-face using the preceding advice. There are many ways to meet like-minded people, whether you attend networking events, take a class, or join a local group. You may widen your social network and even meet someone special with a little work.

Approaching Women with Honor and Confidence

Older guys are generally in a different situation when meeting ladies. On the one hand, they might be more confident and experienced in life than their younger peers. On the other hand, they might think they're too old or out of touch to be dating. The secret to approaching women confidently and respectfully is the same regardless of age.

Making sure you seem attractive and well-groomed is the first step. Men who care for themselves and exude confidence are inherently attractive to women. Don a beautiful outfit, clean your teeth, and ensure that any facial hair is cropped neatly.

Additionally, it's critical to have an approachable and open body language. It will appear as though you are distant or uninterested if you stand or sit with your arms crossed or your head lowered. Instead, keep your posture open and look the woman in the eye.

Now that you've established contact, starting a dialogue is time. Maintain a pleasant and upbeat tone throughout the talk, starting with a joke or remark. Pay close attention to what she says and follow up with questions to demonstrate your curiosity about her. It's also a fantastic opportunity to tell a little about yourself, but try not to give away too much.

Lastly, remember to honor her personal space. Don't push the matter if she shows no desire to talk more or if she puts up any opposition. Often, a courteous "It was nice meeting you" may suffice to finish the conversation.

Older men can approach women with confidence and respect by following these guidelines. By doing this, they will demonstrate that they still possess the skills necessary to succeed in the dating market and raise their chances of meeting the appropriate woman.

Never trust what you read on the internet.

Don't believe everything you read online in 2023. By now, everyone should know better than to trust anything they read online. But many people are duped by false online dating profiles, and when they finally meet someone in person, they are let down. If it's your first time meeting someone, make sure it's in a public place and plan a separate journey for yourself. Even if you might think you know someone well, a computerized association doesn't always imply "this present reality."

Inform Someone Of Your Whereabouts

Since safety is a concern for everyone when we go on dates, it's imperative to let someone know where you are!

Tell the person you're going and what you're doing, regardless of whether you met them via a common friend or a dating app. You may nominate your best friend, brother, or even your mom, from whom you borrowed the sweater. Not only are you safeguarding yourself, but you also have someone you can chat with after the date. Everyone is supported.

5.

Practice asking probing questions and paying attention.

Before you ever meet someone for the first time, you most likely text or message them on an online dating app or website. One way to develop active listening is to pose questions. Alternatively, you might have met in person or through acquaintances; in any case, you've probably spoken to each other before going on a first date!

I understand that it is easy for you to think of funny things to say about yourself, which you can do if the conversation goes off-topic, but try not to! By posing and answering questions, you can steer the conversation toward the other person more. This is what encourages real communication.

We've compiled a list of the most popular queries about online dating in case you need conversation-starter ideas!

The questions "What do you do?" and "What show are you currently binge-watching on Netflix?" are typical ones that you can answer. They are timeless. But take into account other options.

Pay attention to where the conversation is leading you. In your conversation, try to find common ground.

Furthermore, don't worry about taking a few seconds off; sitting in agony is acceptable.

Rephrasing or confirming what they have said can be useful if you truly find it difficult to get up a conversation:
Online dating: Yes, I interned for this NGO in the city. Even though it takes a lot of work, I enjoy it.
"It takes a lot of work," you say.
Online dating: Without a doubt, I oversee a lot of practical work, such as interacting with clients directly. Does that ever happen to you at work?
To create a solid connection, you must trust and be honest with each other. The issue is that people may now blend in behind veneers of all kinds, sophisticated and not. As a result, you should be the one to initiate early contact with any possible partners. Asking your date if they plan to have children or if they've visited an STD testing clinic in the last three months may seem odd, but if those topics are important to you, you should bring them up. Honest relationships are the finest, even though some individuals may find it offensive to be open and honest. In conclusion, don't be scared to be

whoyou are; there is nothing more charming than being yourself.

Chapter 2: Goal-setting

One of the biggest mistakes guys make when selecting a mate is responding impulsively rather than carefully. It's typical for men to have intense feelings of want for visually appealing women visually appealing women, but it's crucial to pause and evaluate whether those requirements align with his desires. For example, a man could be attracted to a woman purely because of her appearance, even though he desires a committed partner and a long-term commitment. A relationship like that could only end in disappointment. But it's unethical for a man to pursue a woman who is seeking emotional connection if he's simply interested in exciting, casual sex.

Because of this, it's essential to approach choosing a partner thoughtfully and clearly regarding your wants and desires. To do this, you should first use Robert Sternberg's triangular theory of love to divide your wants into intimacy, passion, and commitment.[25] One or more of the three factors may be present simultaneously in the urge to draw a lady. Based on these criteria, you may evaluate your attractiveness to a possible spouse. It's crucial to remember that some guys may have a compulsive need for validation from others, which may influence the people they choose as partners. Later in the book, we'll explore this subject in more detail and discuss possible solutions.

2.1. Closeness

Our innate urge to be near those similar to ourselves for comfort, reproduction, and survival lies at the basis of our emotional requirement for intimacy. Every aspect of human interaction, including thinking about a loved one and physical touch like massages, kisses, hugs, and sex, can evoke this closeness.[26][27]

Although the need for sex is a sign of both connection and passion, it should only be viewed as the pinnacle of closeness in this situation rather than the basis of a relationship. It's important to reframe the need for proximity as a reason for choosing a spouse based on personality traits, common interests, and passions rather than physical appearance. These elements will establish whether or not a lady is a good fit for a committed, emotionally satisfying relationship.

Diminishing the significance of sexual desire

the first impulse to own a lady, which is frequently connected to their sexual desire. In turn, the primary sexual urge is frequently linked to a woman's physical attractiveness. But it's vital to understand that a woman's physical appeal does not always translate into her attributes, essential for creating a deep and enduring connection. Even though a lady who looks good on the outside might not have what it takes for a closeness-based relationship, it's still possible. Trying to mold her into the person you want her to be will ultimately end in disappointment. Therefore, when looking for a mate for a

good relationship, it's crucial to stress human qualities over exterior attributes. Some things need to be taken into account to minimize the importance of sexual desire. Comprehending these elements can boost the drive to give priority to more significant attributes:
• Studies and surveys have shown that social standing and physical attractiveness are typically valued before a relationship starts. However, once a relationship begins, appearance and sexuality naturally take a backseat as attention turns to other attributes required for emotional connection.[28][29]

• When you get what you want, your desire to get a lady diminishes because it was originally motivated by novelty. The Coolidge effect is a phenomenon that has been well investigated. In essence, males usually reserve their level of sexual desire for when potential mates show up. With every successive sexual act, the urge to mate with the same partner diminishes until it vanishes entirely if they are still together. It takes time for the desire to return after that.[30][31]

• Whether or not a lady initially piques our interest sexually, spending time with her invariably results in emotional attachment. It takes time to experience a closeness and emotional bond. These emotions result from ongoing interaction and the proximity effect, which is based on the mere exposure effect.[16][17] As a result, the first decision is not impartial because outside variables, including sexual desire, influenced it.

• It is possible to deliberately cultivate sexual desire, especially if both parties are interested in it. A sensation of intimacy, a sense of novelty, an increase in adrenaline from pushing boundaries, and direct sexual touch are the foundations of sexual desire. At the very least, we don't feel close until we start touching each other. We don't appreciate its significance unless we have complete interaction. When we advance in our sexual skills and add something fresh to the relationship, we experience a sense of novelty. By growing sexual interpersonal experience and discovering new aspects of one another. We'll go into greater detail about these issues in the "Sex" chapter.

Chapter 1: Let's get started

What are you trying to find?

Although it might appear clear, it isn't. Although there are many other kinds of relationships, I'll focus on four[JL3] categories to help you limit your options: fiancé, friend with benefits, fuck buddy, or financial sponsor. Allow me to simply explain each so you may comprehend them better.

Fuck My Friend

Sex over friendship is the fundamental component of this relationship. Put simply, the fact that you both have sex is the reason you get along. You shouldn't be concerned if you don't see him for a while. You also don't care if your friend calls alone near your hometown.

A beneficial friend

Work this out! You enjoy hanging out, playing games, getting drinks, and doing all the other things that friends do. You have this friend. Furthermore, you decide to add sex to the list to liven up your friendship. This implies that even after the sex ceases, you stay close friends. Recall that there are no expectations or romantic commitments.

Being an FWB sounds like the ideal solution for girls who struggle with commitment, at least theoretically. Why is this the case? Because even when there isn't any sex involved, you are sleeping with a guy you like, trust, and love spending time with. In contrast to fuck buddies, FWB have an amazing friendship and only occasionally have sex.

Being a friend with benefits is preferable to being a fuck buddy, in my opinion. That female who detests pointless sex is me. I enjoy a little cheeky behavior when I'm having sex. I adore talking to people after sex. I enjoy being vulnerable. This is only feasible if the other person is someone you click with and who shares your most intense dreams and deepest wants.

Since I've been there, I'll also tell you what usually goes wrong in a relationship of this kind. As with any other relationship, feelings may surface eventually, and you may find yourself inadvertently invading each other's personal space. Jealousy can surface, particularly if one of the participants chooses to move on and find love elsewhere. When you both become emotionally involved and unintentionally fall in love with one another, that's another strange situation. If you're not careful, these problems could wreck your personal life if handled tactfully.

Sponsor financially

Sponsorship is nothing new. It has existed there for all of recorded history. When our grandmothers were growing up, parents would find a sponsor for their daughters, who would later be married off when they reached adulthood.

The times have changed, and we can now select the sponsors we want.

However, precisely who is a financial sponsor?

A sponsor is typically an older, wealthy man who supports a lovely young girl's lifestyle; he may be married or widower. However, it's not unusual to see middle-aged and older women also receiving sponsorships.

There is always a trade-off in this type of partnership, and a precise agreement between the parties is necessary. Well, a pampered existence in return for cozy companionship with a youthful, exuberant spirit.

This is the perfect partnership for you if your aim in life is to experience everything to the maximum. You can now own costly automobiles, eat at fancy restaurants, travel and shop overseas, own opulent homes, drive fancy cars, and indulge in everything you dare to love. Alright, whatever! To obtain what you desire, do whatever it takes.

Though, it's not all sunshine and roses. In life, you might have to make certain compromises. An older man isn't likely to lead an exciting, flexible life that would allow him to devote all his valuable time to your hobbies. He will probably think that going out and partying every night is juvenile.

Additionally, an older guy is more inclined to "father" you in a way that could come out as overbearing. He has, after all, far more experience and accomplishments than you could ever hope to have.

To put it plainly, once you determine this is the type of relationship you want, you'll need to be incredibly resilient. Your peers may make fun of you and treat you unfairly. They're more inclined to think of you as a gold-digger and your partner as an elderly pervert who only needs your youthful blood to satiate his needs.

fiance

Or ought I to refer to him as my life mate? This is probably the perfect companion for you—a committed man with whom you can see yourself in a long-term relationship that will hopefully result in marriage and starting a family. Correct?

You should know that this relationship is a costly gift you cannot just purchase. It takes time to mature. And if you want that ring on your finger, you'll have to give up time and effort. Hi there!

Where To Look For Love

Do you want to discover how to become more confident around the other sex and enhance the likelihood that you will hit on a flirtation? Steer clear of the typical mistake of approaching someone you like before asking if you can flirt with them. Adopting a more calculated stance is essential for successful flirtation.

There are plenty of options for you to enjoy exploring as you hone your flirting skills when you look at the classic flirting grounds and explore some new ones in addition to flirting blind.

It needs at least two players to play flirting. It's one thing to learn from a book, but you must go out there and flirt in person. Justifications like "you don't know anyone you want to flirt with" or "you never meet new people" are insufficient. Some locations where you can meet single people to flirt with are included in the following categories.

Evident Locations

Don't give up if you work alone in a small office; you still have suppliers, clients, and others to flirt with. On the other hand, if you work in a large or shared facility, the office kitchen, smokers' corner, vending machine area, and building entrance are important locations to look for singletons.

In general, flirting in bars is less awkward than in a grocery store or church since patrons there are more likely to be approached in this lively social setting.

Remember the following:

Finding the correct kind of singletons starts with selecting the best bar for you. Avoid sports pubs that transmit live TV if, for example, football isn't your thing. Seek a location with a reputation for safety and a mixed clientele of people in your age range. Seek recommendations from people who seem similar to you if you are unfamiliar with the area.

• Bars are the fastest place for flirting, so follow the crowd and don't be shy. Someone will immediately clarify that they don't want to be approached by not making eye contact, smiling, or engaging in conversation. Some people may even turn or angle away from you to make it clear that they are not interested in flirting with you.

Other Locations

Don't confine your flirting to the obvious venues, like the workplace or clubs; flirtation can happen anywhere people assemble.

Other locations where flirting is acceptable include, but are not limited to:

• Hotels – other patrons, bar and restaurant employees; • Planes, trains, and cars – other commuters and other passengers; • Supermarkets – checkout personnel and other consumers;

It's not impossible to flirt with a commuter, but generally, only if you're passing someone you don't know. When they see someone they know, commuters usually don't initiate conversation for fear that they won't like them and will have to avoid or chat with them for years to come.

Regular commuters sometimes strike up conversations that lead to marriage, but you can read the indications to determine whether someone is interested in talking to you.

• Parks: any more parkgoers, including families and dog walkers.
• Other members of the gym.
• Anywhere a group assembles or a congregation is present, such as during a demonstration, a sporting event, a social gathering after church, a band or choir practice, or the beach.

It could take longer to get someone's attention when you approach them subtly in an unexpected setting, unlike bars where patrons anticipate being approached. It is your responsibility to take action in these cases.

A pleasant flirtation can take you places you never imagined or introduce you to someone. The theory that there are only six degrees of separation between you and everyone on the earth may be familiar to you. Everyone on the earth is essentially only six steps away from each other if you're one step away from everyone you know and two steps away from everyone you know. It then follows that your ideal flirting is just a few steps away from you.

Online

There are countless options to meet individuals worldwide on the Internet. Three factors make flirting online faster and more daring than flirting in person:

Face-to-face rejection is not a risk, and physical chemistry is unimportant.
• You can be more straightforward, explicit, and obvious about your objectives using written language instead of nonverbal cues.

Use a reputable website like www.match.com to try your hand at online flirting. If you like someone's page on a social networking site like Facebook, you can ask a buddy to introduce you to them virtually.

There are many options for online flirting in forums and chat rooms; everybody can find the specialty they're looking for. On the www.LinkedIn.com forum, professionals can connect with other professionals. Along with expanding your virtual network, you're also establishing relationships with individuals who share your interests.

In contrast to dating websites, you can be confident that the individuals you meet in chat rooms and forums have something in common even though you can't ensure they are single or seeking.

It takes skill to use language correctly, and it matters a lot to do so when flirting.

Remember the following:

• Spelling and grammar errors can turn people off since they may assume you're unintelligent. Always proofread your message before submitting it, even if you wrote quickly.
• Excessive flirting could be taken as an indication that you want to have sex with the person. Be playful and lighthearted when flirting online. You must keep their interest in asking them out on a first date.
• Your best friend while flirting online is humor. Being hilarious is a lot easier for some people when it's written down; there's no awkward, quiet, or polite laughing if the other person doesn't find what you're saying funny.

- Don't stress about composing lengthy messages; most recipients can determine whether they appreciate your writing style in a few phrases. It's just as effective to compliment someone on their photo or writing style online as in person.
- Always provide a recent photo of yourself, and use a seductive screen name only if you're ready for others to reach out to you.

Chapter 4: The Captain of Her Emotional Ship

This brings us to the last section of the text game mastery. Using precise language to pique her interest.

I ask that you do yourself a favor and ensure you truly understand this idea. Visit the Amazon Kindle Store page right now. Check out all of the top sellers. Romantic novels will make up 75% of what you view.

Why?

BECAUSE IT'S PORN FOR GIRLS To see some expert wordplay, I'd strongly advise getting a copy of a best-selling free romance novel from the free section.

It's not because of these nonsense tales of some guy wooing a girl that makes them think it's porn. This is because romance novelists give readers an orgasm through their writing by using highly descriptive keywords!

As a marketer, I was aware of the popularity of romantic novels. I researched it and read a few books to see whether using those principles might make a woman fall in love with you! Yes, that is the response.

But the trick is to do this without appearing overly assertive too soon. Ideally, you should attempt using these strategies after you've been messaging someone for a short while or if you had sex with them in person before even exchanging numbers.

Idea #1: Sexual Phrases: Women Are Not Exempt From Dirty Minds!

I'm not sure why men believe that women are some kind of non-human animal. Almost many guys approach women with the mindset that it's wrong to reveal your feelings to them, making them the object of their affection. Did you intend to tiptoe forever?

Most guys assume she calls them out when the girls eventually realize you're flirting.

Change your perspective so that you are leading her instead of thinking of it as you tiptoeing until she gives you the go-ahead. Establishing a foundation of trust and advancing the partnership properly by taking baby steps. I assure you that she wants to give you a chance if you're a good guy. However, she needs to gain confidence and get to know and interact with you in various contexts.

You have to get rid of the tiptoe mentality and acknowledge that women desire sex just as much, if not more than men do.

Because she has a similarly filthy mind, finding ingenious methods to introduce sexual phrases will drive her to think about, you guessed it, sexual things.

"I'll email you a picture of the crazy lambo I saw having sex today."

"whoops during a sexual encounter."

What the heck is autocorrect doing?
"sec" means "finally."
She is thinking of you right now because she is reading your text message. Additionally, she has seen the word "sex" THREE times.
Her thoughts quickly turn to the next thing and the races. And you've managed to avoid coming across as a creep at all.
"You'll be happy to hear that I got that haircut at last."
"Fuck it" or "I always leave my man Steve a great tit."
"TIP" and "wow"
Her thoughts are racing after yet another ridiculous example, "FUCK TIT." Oh, and she might laugh at it since it's quite humorous.
Consider that. Laughter combined with sexual thoughts opens the floodgates to accepting and receiving such thoughts. Ideas that you shared with her.
She's processing you + funny + sexual in her brain.

Selecting A Date

Now that you have established ground rules for yourself, it's time to locate someone for you. The dating scene has advanced significantly in recent years. Unlike when it was limited to people in the same circle and with common friends, there are now various options to go out there and find your ideal date. People search for breadth and diversity, which they frequently scope in a bigger context. Numerous options are available, including double dating, casual dating, blind dating, speed dating, and internet dating.

A specific dating service or group typically organizes speed dating. Before the event officially begins, people register. They visit a spot, a bar, or a restaurant and hang out with other potential dates. The average encounter lasts between five and ten minutes. This type of date greatly depends on first impressions, but it also allows the applicant to meet other people and determine the best fit for them.

Speed dating benefits those who wish to develop their conversational and social abilities because it teaches you those things. Additionally, since you will be conversing with strangers a lot on these dates, this is ideal for those who are at ease meeting new people and do not bother to strike up a discussion. This dating style will not be successful for you if you are an introvert.

Online dating is the practice of meeting individuals through the internet. By way of the internet, both sides learn to know one another. This 21st-century dating approach was made possible by a plethora of dating applications. This is incredibly convenient for couples from different towns or even different countries. Eventually, after making a deep connection, the two will get together to advance to a more committed relationship.

Nowadays, most people—especially those constantly on the go—prefer online dating. This one involves less preparation time and is affordable compared to other dating styles. This is advantageous for those who are inherently bashful because it prevents you from conversing with someone in person, thanks to the screen in front of you. However, because you can never be certain of the person's identity on the other side of the screen, this kind of dating can also be a little risky. Be extremely cautious when speaking to others because some people are dishonest.

When two strangers are arranged to meet for a date by mutual friends, family, or coworkers, it's known as blind dating. They act as a sort of go-between for the two groups. "blind date" refers to a situation where neither of you knows the other's appearance. But occasionally, the matchmaker gives you a general indication about each other, such as your physical characteristics and shared interests.

Those who are thrill-seekers and highly adventurous should consider blind dating. This heightens the thrill that comes with dating. It's common for "love at first sight" to occur on blind dates, and you never know—your love tale might be destined for this. On blind dates, though, try not to have too high expectations because you can despise the person for not living up to your expectations—at least not in terms of appearance.

Casual dating is the practice of dating numerous people. It can involve both parties or simply one of them. People who aren't ready to settle down date this kind of dating because it doesn't involve promises or commitments. People interested in casual dating often have the mentality of "seeing what the world can offer me." In this manner, when he or she meets the "right one," they might explore other options before settling down with him or her. Or, worst-case scenario, for those without the desire to settle down.

But once you start a connection of this nature, you must exercise extreme caution. Casual dating typically translates into casual sex. Ensure you're prepared for a relationship with little to no sentiments because you might desire something more once you start feeling anything for your date. If your date feels the same, you're in luck; if not, you're in trouble.

Two couples going out together is known as double dating. The younger dating environment is rife with situations like this. This kind of date allows both couples to speak with each other and start a conversation. This date is typically chosen when one or both couples have recently begun to hang together. They can prevent embarrassing moments when the discussion dwindles by doing this. It also lets you observe how your date behaves around other people.

Chapter 5: Adding Flavor

Starting a new relationship is a thrilling experience full of joy, excitement, and the expectation of meeting someone wonderful. Even if the initial stages are frequently defined by the excitement of getting to know one another, maintaining the flame throughout time is crucial. This book intends to help you keep the flame of desire burning brightly in your new relationship by enabling you to keep the spark and spice things up.

Spend time communicating your needs, wants, and expectations to your partner honestly and openly. Talk about your hopes and dreams as well as your worries and anxieties. This will establish a more profound emotional bond and pave the way for a more satisfying partnership.

Astonishment and Joy:

Bring spontaneity into your relationship by catching your lover off guard with kind acts. It may be as easy as putting together a surprise date, sending a thoughtful note, or organizing a weekend getaway. These unplanned gestures of affection can rekindle the passion for romance and convey to your significant other your appreciation and value.

Find Common Interests:

Develop common interests and pastimes to make your relationship stronger. Participating in activities as a pair forges enduring memories and deepens your bond, whether cooking together, taking up a new sport, or discovering a hobby. You will feel united in this shared experience, which will maintain the vitality of your relationship.

Maintain the Romance:

Never undervalue the impact that romantic gestures can have. Adding romance to your relationship can help you keep that closeness, whether through candlelit dinners or a casual stroll outside under the stars. The romance will endure and deepen your emotional bond with one another if you have regular date nights, thoughtful presents, and displays of affection.

Accept Unpredictability:

In your relationship, embrace unpredictability and break out from monotony. Try new activities with your partner, like driving an unexpected road trip, learning a new skill, or dining at a new restaurant. Accepting the unexpected keeps things exciting and guarantees your relationship will always be new and exciting.

Put Quality Time First:

It is important to make time for your partner amid the daily chaos. Spending time with each other enhances your relationship. It serves as a reminder of the happiness of being together, whether over a weekend away or a quiet night watching movies.

Preserve Your Uniqueness:

Maintaining separate identities is just as crucial as forging a deep bond. Promote personal development and follow your interests outside of relationships. This guarantees that you both keep developing as people and gives your relationship more depth. Maintaining the spark in the exciting journey of a new relationship calls for work, ingenuity, and a dedication to fostering your bond. You can ensure your relationship stays alive and keeps growing by valuing open communication, developing common interests, and adding romance into your everyday life. So add some spice to your relationship and set out on a passionate and lasting voyage of love.

It usually does not play well for an imagination that leads partners to believe they would prefer to be the one to convert the lover.

If a single religious practice is never decided upon, this could limit the love affair's ability to grow to an unfavorable degree and ultimately cause a serious scenario to take root.

Recognize that when two individuals date, they are moving as one unit; issues that tend to impede this effect should be examined and resolved.

The fact that there is a conflict of purpose and neither partner is prepared to make concessions for the other is another major problem impacting dating as two people start living together.

For example, one partner might want to start a business, while the other might not want anything and think that no commercial venture should be established.

When the time comes for him or her to support the partner, he or she may do so by withholding resources. Usually, it kills an enthusiastic entrepreneur's ambition because the person they must look up to would not support them.

Another situation involves a guy and a woman who, before dating, are both working on extremely difficult assignments. This would make it impossible to concentrate on any intended project since you could never be sure when someone else would provide a helping hand.

A compromise to collaborate as a team should be encouraged to progress in a relationship. Generally speaking, women are told to see past a man's vision and back him to his goal.

It is, therefore, essential that a male, before committing to a woman, ensure that she is aware of his goals and projects. Nevertheless, ambitious women in the 21st century work on noteworthy initiatives and goals. If a man who wants to date someone has this kind of woman in mind, he is advised to play a supportive role in maintaining the relationship if possible.

Take Initiative Rather Than Reacting

Start acting like the "man" she wants you to be if you have a female you're attracted to. Have the guts to go up to her and extend an invitation. The worst thing she could do is refuse. You two will either click, or you'll move on to another female, but I promise you the world will still be turning. Someone you like and deserving of all your affection is that person.

There are only two possible outcomes, and neither involves the cosmos collapsing. Give up hoping for the "stars to align themselves" or things to "just go your way." Achievers are different from dreamers in that they know when to give up on their dreams and begin putting them into action.

It's easy to justify being reactive and waiting for your gal to fall into your lap. There are a lot of justifications in this position that allow you to avoid admitting that you're giving in. Meanwhile, while you're making excuses like "the time isn't right" and "well, now that she's got a boyfriend and I can't possibly say anything now," some slick playboy will show up and win your girl over. You can't damn it, but that's only because someone else had her before you did.

And even if you believe she could not say "yes" in any case, remember the fundamental truth that, regardless of your self-perception, your odds of landing her were precisely 50%. What separates a "yes" from a "no"? There are just two possible answers.

Sixth Dating Advice: Don't Ever Be A Tool

If you give your best for someone else's meager efforts, you will never advance, no matter how hard you try to better yourself. Reverse the situation: you wouldn't be all that interested in a girl who offered you everything in return for the smallest amount of work on your part. Would she inspire you to put in more effort or improve yourself for her sake? Most likely not, as it's difficult to appreciate someone willing to put up such little effort.

Thus, establish some limits and maintain them! Refrain from interrupting your current task to hastily approach another person and engage in small talk about their problems or feelings. You must overcome the illusion of being a "knight in shining armor." Being a helpful "tool" for someone else's problems is the easiest way to get your friends banned from your circle.

Therefore, you can answer calls from the female you like if you keep them brief and explicitly state that they are during your time, whether for yourself, your friends, or your interests. Then, immediately return to your previous task. Of course, in the event of a true emergency, you can assist.

The lesson here is that why should anyone else respect your needs and boundaries if you don't value them enough to consider them? Indeed, many men enjoy being hopeless romantics and giving their partners all they could ask for. However, you must figure out how to accomplish it without losing credibility. And only after you've acquired them, even then. What's the difference if you treat your girlfriend the same way you would a female friend you're crushing on? The two must be distinguished from one another.

Make time and space for your interests and activities even after you start dating. Respect your partner's time and space with the same decency. The amusing thing is that if you both engage in sedentary activities, you could sit in the same room and enjoy your "me" moments. But never completely disregard oneself for the benefit of another. Years from now, the two of you will still be grateful that you did.

Anyway, what is marriage all about?

A while back, I was asked, "What is the difference between a wedding and a marriage?" by someone. Although it can sound the same to some, it is not. The marriage ceremony honors the joining of two individuals in holy matrimony. Additionally, it is the location where two people make the covenant of marriage, which is a lifetime commitment.

Being married is more than just agreeing to live together for as long as it makes both of you happy. It is a covenant that lasts until death. It denotes your commitment to accompany this individual on life's path through thick and thin, good times and bad, joyful moments and sorrowful moments. It implies that you cannot abandon the ship when things get too hot. You must persevere through to the very end. You may decide to divorce in some circumstances, such as when your partner is abusive. However, the goal of the separation should be to create room for therapy and healing to facilitate reunion.

God's Design for Marriage

Adam did not propose marriage. Adam didn't even realize what was lacking in his life until the Lord clarified it. Following his statement that it was bad for a man to live alone, God had a man give names to every animal (Genesis 2:18–20). Adam had previously found satisfaction in God for everything. He was unaware that he needed assistance.

He most likely started to notice that there was a female animal for every male when he gave the animals names. It was a sign from God that he needed something.

Possibly, he experienced an awakening and realized he was alone. In an attempt to locate his spouse, he must have started to watch attentively any animal that approached him for naming. Given that verse 20 states, "But for Adam no suitable helper was found" (NIV), he must have been searching. The word "found" suggests that he searched.

When the moment for marriage arrives, I've discovered that the realization that you are by yourself hits hard. You start searching for your partner among the crowds of people you encounter daily for some reason. Every day, no matter where you are—at the grocery store, coffee shop, or church—you unconsciously scan the other sex for your partner.

God answered Adam's longing by putting him to sleep and constructing a woman for him out of his ribs. When he was finished, he gave her to him. Adam discovered that his female was not among those that he had listed. Adam knew right away who his mate was.

After God made Adam aware of his need, he began to long for a partner, and God provided him with a suitable companion created especially for him. It still operates in this manner now. God has a spouse for you if you have discovered that you are craving a partner. Your heart's desire signifies someone is out there for you to marry. If God gave you the desire for a partner but did not grant you that partner, that would be cruel—and our God is not evil!

We can infer the following lessons from this tale:

God was the one who proposed this first marriage. He was the one who realized Adam was better off with a partner and that being alone was not healthy for him. God decided that Adam and Eve should get married. This thought did not occur to Adam.

It was God who determined what kind of partner Adam should have. Adam had no idea what a good assistant should look like or what characteristics made her a good match for him.

God got to work getting his partner ready for him.

After creating his wife, God did not send Adam out to find her. He showed her to him.

God has already predetermined this relationship's structure. "For this reason, a man will join his wife and become one flesh, leaving behind his parents." Genesis 2:14 (NIV) They would become one from this moment forward.

Selecting a partner would be considerably simpler with God's blessings if we could only adhere to those guidelines.

First rookie error

When you were out on a date, did the woman ever offer to pay for the drinks? While at the register, she may have even taken out her bank card, but you say, "I'll get these; don't worry about it." Close your card," or perhaps something a little more animated, like "No! No! Don't worry - what are you doing? I'll obtain it!

By the way, this may apply to practically anything in life, such as a request for a gift or a compliment. A recurring scenario is when the woman offers to pay for the beverages, but we wave her hand and offer to pay instead. It may appear heroic or extremely gentlemanly at first, but we are often just attempting to do something "nice."

However, we aren't acting kindly. She is feeling wounded by us. The days of guys purchasing everything are long gone.

Allow a woman to buy you something when she wants to, like the next round of drinks! Don't try to stop her. Never even say to her, "Oh, that's very kind of you." Behaving as though everything was normal. Act as though you are constantly being bought out. Go so far as to anticipate it.

Shopping by women is a positive thing.

You want her to put some money into the relationship; she can do this by purchasing beverages for the next conversation round. You effectively prevent her from investing in the conversation if you prevent her from purchasing the beverages. Remember that when it comes to business, people value the things to which they have committed time, money, and other resources. She is investing more money the more she purchases. She values you more the more she invests.

Rarely do women continue to follow outdated customs. What am I referring to? Here's where the woman assumes full financial responsibility for the man. Such a woman would freely express her opinions, saying things like, "Of course, a man is supposed to pay for everything," when you meet her.

In my experience, there are just two occasions like this. Furthermore, their personalities weren't as strong on those dates; while they were attractive outside, they lacked charisma. It's noteworthy to notice that they were both lamenting their inability to locate a suitable partner. Why, I wonder?

If you do encounter these women, exercise caution. They won't feel sorry if you continue to buy everything and spend all your money on them.

Fortunately, these ladies make up a small minority. The majority of women are glad to contribute, which is beneficial.

Declare, "Next round of drinks is on you," without fear, better still if you're wealthy! Here's where your wealth becomes an asset rather than a liability. Let's give it a tiny boost. Assume you are a multimillionaire and take a date to a neighborhood pub. You approach the bar, place your drink order, grin and say, "First round is on me," to her. Or, "It's my turn first, you get 100 on the next round." This will appeal to women because you're not attempting to impress them with your wealth. Should you endeavor to do that, you can insist on purchasing everything. In the worst situation, you start purchasing her pricey toys because you are wealthy and can afford to buy her much more than just beverages.

www.ingramcontent.com/pod-product-compliance
Lightning Source LLC
Chambersburg PA
CBHW052154110526
44591CB00012B/1961